WITHDRAWN

FRANKLIN PARK PUBLIC LIBRARY

FRANKLIN PARK, IL.

Each borrower is held responsible for all library
material drawn on his card and for fines accruing on
the same. No material will be issued until such fine
has been paid.

All injuries to library material beyond reasonable
wear and all losses shall be made good to the
satisfaction of the Librarian.

Replacement costs will be
billed after 42 days overdue.

George Lucas

Filmmaker & Creator of *Star Wars*

by Grace Hansen

Abdo
HISTORY MAKER
BIOGRAPHIES
Kids

J-B
LUCAS
455-0888

abdopublishing.com

Published by Abdo Kids, a division of ABDO, P.O. Box 398166, Minneapolis, Minnesota 55439.

Copyright © 2018 by Abdo Consulting Group, Inc. International copyrights reserved in all countries. No part of this book may be reproduced in any form without written permission from the publisher.

Printed in the United States of America, North Mankato, Minnesota.

102017

012018

 THIS BOOK CONTAINS RECYCLED MATERIALS

Photo Credits: AP Images, Getty Images, iStock, Seth Poppel/Yearbook Library, Shutterstock © Unknown/Modesto Bee/ZUMAPRESS.com p.11

Production Contributors: Teddy Borth, Jennie Forsberg, Grace Hansen

Design Contributors: Dorothy Toth, Laura Mitchell

Publisher's Cataloging in Publication Data

Names: Hansen, Grace, author.

Title: George Lucas: filmmaker & creator of Star Wars / by Grace Hansen.

Other titles: Filmmaker & creator of Star Wars | Filmmaker and creator of Star Wars

Description: Minneapolis, Minnesota : Abdo Kids, 2018. | Series: History maker biographies | Includes glossary, index and online resource (page 24).

Identifiers: LCCN 2017943141 | ISBN 9781532104251 (lib.bdg.) | ISBN 9781532105371 (ebook) | ISBN 9781532105937 (Read-to-me ebook)

Subjects: LCSH: Lucas, George, 1944- --Juvenile literature. | Motion picture producers and directors--United States--Biography--Juvenile literature. | Star Wars films--Juvenile literature.

Classification: DDC 791.43023 [B]--dc23

LC record available at https://lccn.loc.gov/2017943141

Table of Contents

Early Life

George Walton Lucas Jr. was born on May 14, 1944. He grew up in a small town near Modesto, California.

California

From a young age, Lucas loved reading and drawing. He also loved cars and racing. He dreamed of being a race car driver. That changed after a bad car accident in high school.

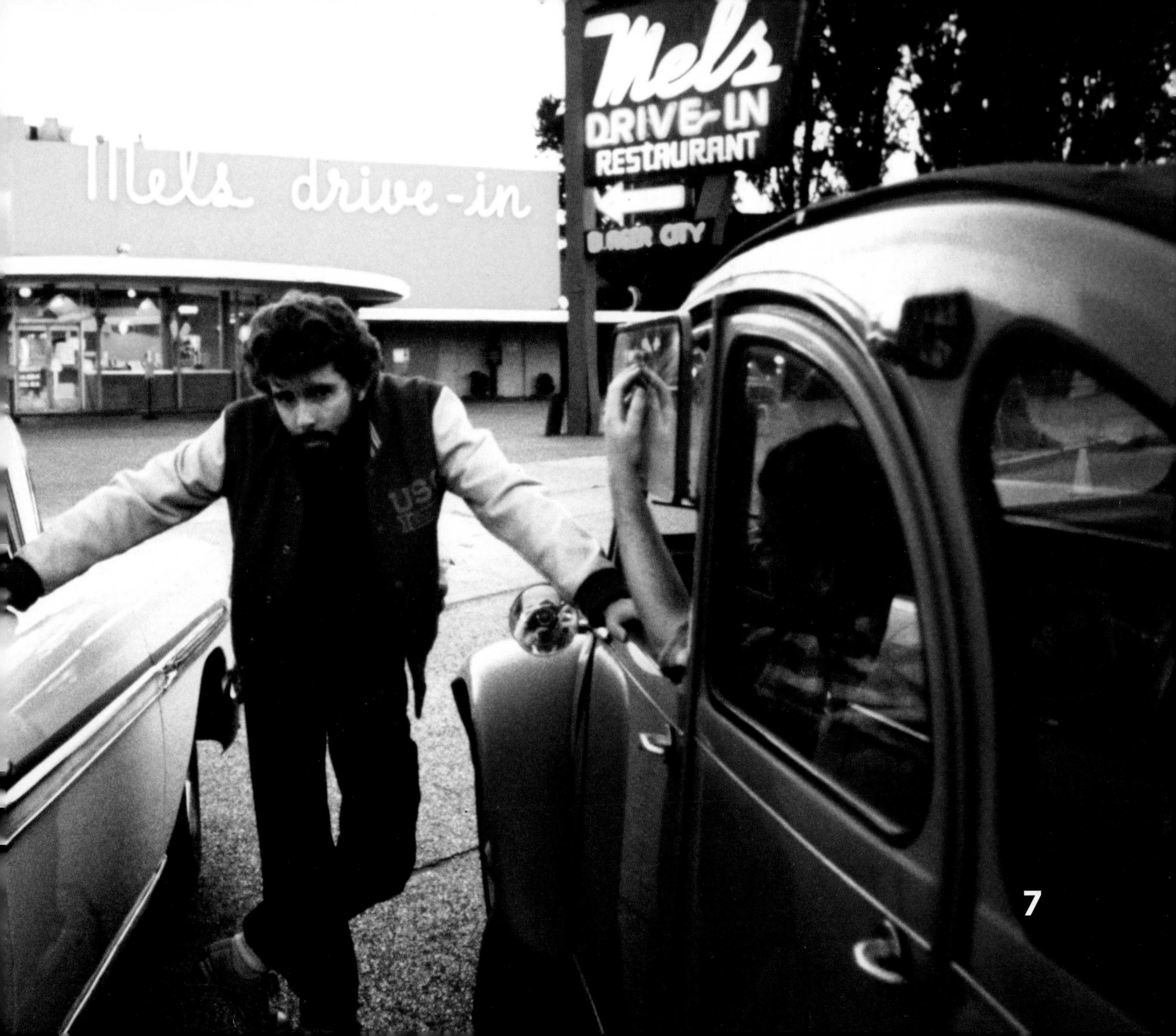
Mels drive-in
Mels
DRIVE-IN
RESTAURANT

Lucas later went to community college. He found a passion for film. Lucas transferred to USC. He studied cinematography and graduated in 1966.

His film work in college earned him attention. In 1967, Warner Brothers gave Lucas an **internship**. He learned how to direct on movie sets.

First Films

In 1971, Lucas released his first full-length film. It was called *THX 1138*. It did not do well, but Lucas did not give up.

13

He went on to write and direct *American Graffiti*. The movie was a huge success. It was **nominated** for 5 Academy Awards.

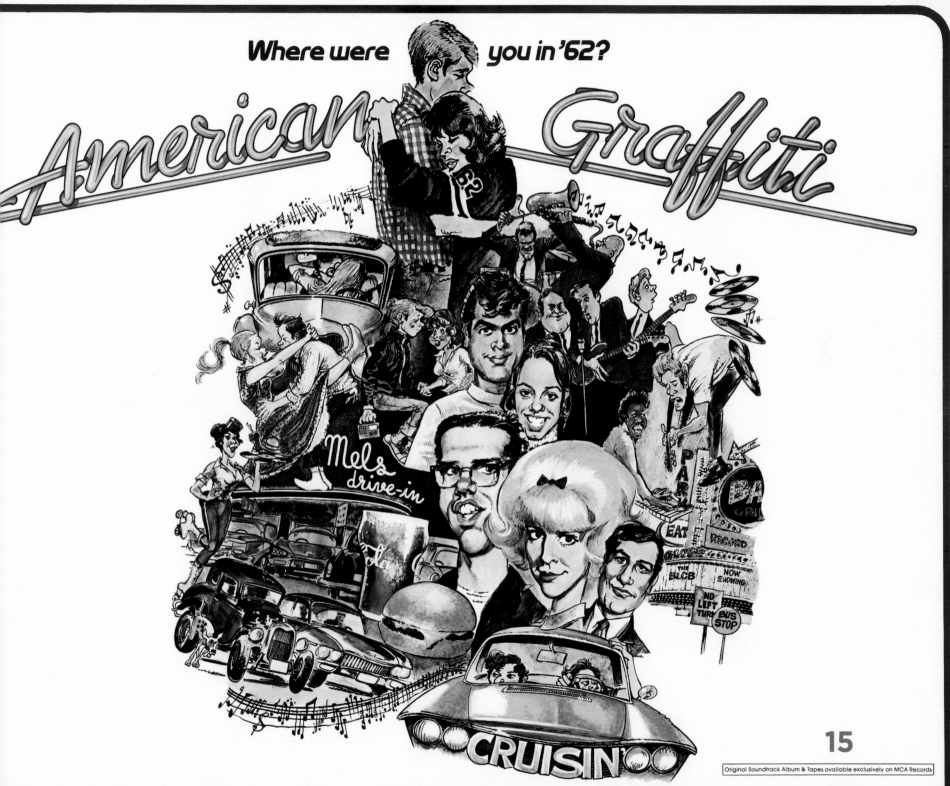

Where were you in '62?

American Graffiti

15

N GRAFFITI" • A LUCASFILM LTD./COPPOLA CO. Production • Starring RICHARD DREYFUSS • RONNY HOWARD • PAUL LE MAT • CHARLIE MARTIN SMITH • CANDY CLARK • MACKENZIE PHILLIPS • CINDY WILLIAMS • WOLFMAN JACK
GEORGE LUCAS and GLORIA KATZ & WILLARD HUYCK • Directed by GEORGE LUCAS • Co-Produced by GARY KURTZ • Produced by FRANCIS FORD COPPOLA • A UNIVERSAL PICTURE • TECHNICOLOR®
PG PARENTAL GUIDANCE SUGGESTED SOME MATERIAL MAY NOT BE SUITABLE FOR PRE-TEENAGERS

Star Wars!

Lucas's next project would be his greatest. He released *Star Wars* in 1977. It had special effects that viewers had never seen before. The film won 7 Academy Awards!

Two more Star Wars films were released in 1980 and 1983. Lucas created another series within that time. It featured adventurer Indiana Jones.

On To New Adventures

More Star Wars films came
out in 1999, 2002, and 2005.
Lucas soon decided he was
done with big movies. His
focus is now on smaller
movies and his family.

21

Timeline

George graduates from the University of Southern California.

American Graffiti, written and directed by Lucas, is released in August.

Lucas adopts daughter Amanda. He later adopts two more children. His fourth child, with wife Mellody, is born in 2013.

1966

1973

1981

1944

1967

1977

1999

May 14
George Walton Lucas Jr. is born in Modesto, California.

George works as an **intern** at Warner Brothers.

Star Wars: A New Hope debuts in theaters. *The Empire Strikes Back* is released in 1980, followed by *Return of the Jedi* in 1983.

Three more Star Wars movies come out between 1999 and 2005.

Glossary

cinematography – the art of making motion pictures.

internship – the position of a student or trainee who works, sometimes without pay, to gain experience.

nominated – formally entered for an honor or award.

USC – an abbreviation for University of Southern California.

Index

Abdo Kids ONLINE

FREE! ONLINE MULTIMEDIA RESOURCES

Visit **abdokids.com** and use this code to access crafts, games, videos, and more!

Abdo Kids Code:
HGK4251